First World War
and Army of Occupation
War Diary
France, Belgium and Germany

33 DIVISION
19 Infantry Brigade
Cameronians (Scottish Rifles)
6th Battalion
1 June 1916 - 10 August 1916

WO95/2422/4

The Naval & Military Press Ltd
www.nmarchive.com
Published in association with The National Archives

Published by

The Naval & Military Press Ltd

Unit 10 Ridgewood Industrial Park,

Uckfield, East Sussex,

TN22 5QE England

Tel: +44 (0) 1825 749494

www.naval-military-press.com

www.nmarchive.com

This diary has been reprinted in facsimile from the original. Any imperfections are inevitably reproduced and the quality may fall short of modern type and cartographic standards.

© Crown Copyright
Images reproduced by permission of The National Archives, London, England, 2015.

Contents

Document type	Place/Title	Date From	Date To
Heading	WO95/2422-4 6 Bn Cameronians (Royal Scottish Rgt) 1915 Dec-1918 Sept		
Heading	33 Division 19 Brig Ade 1/6 Bn Scottish Rifles (Cameronians) 1916 June-1917 Jan.		
War Diary		01/06/1916	01/07/1916
Heading	Lorc. War Diary 1/6th Battn. The Cameronians (Scottish Rifles). July 1916		
War Diary		02/07/1916	30/07/1916
War Diary		01/08/1916	10/08/1916
War Diary			
Miscellaneous	O.C. Reinforcement	19/01/1917	19/01/1917
Miscellaneous	D.A.A.G. Reinforcements	21/01/1917	21/01/1917
Miscellaneous	Base Commandant Staples		
Miscellaneous	D.A.G. G.H.Q. 3rd Echelon Forward.	23/01/1917	23/01/1917
Miscellaneous	AAG L of C		
Miscellaneous	The A.T & 2.m. 18th 2nd R.A.D	22/01/1917	22/01/1917

WO 95 2422/4

6 Bn Cameronians (Royal Scottish Rfls)

1915 Dec - 1918 Sept

33 DIVISION

19 BRIGADE

1/6 BN SCOTTISH RIFLES (CAMERONIANS)

1916 JUNE – 1917 JAN.

FROM 51 DIV – 154 BDE

Amalgamated with 5 BN

WAR DIARY
or INTELLIGENCE SUMMARY

Army Form C. 2118

1/6 Scottish Rifles

Place	Date	Hour	Summary of Events and Information	Remarks and references to Appendices
G.H.Q.	1.6.16 Thursday		The Subalterns, Officers, Warrant Officers, and N.C.O's at East Africa paraded for instruction on the Lewis Guns. A Lewis School for Subalterns was held in the afternoon. The N.C.O. and Officers was held in the evening. The Adjutant went to G.H.Q. to see later per place in — — to N.O. to p.m. 29. Bgd. The day was warm.	
	Friday 2nd June		Officers, N.C.O's and men of A and B Coys paraded under the M.G.O. for instruction in the Lewis Gun, and the Officers, N.C.O's and men of C and D Coys paraded under the Grenadier Officer for instruction in Grenades. The Scouting Section paraded for Flag drill and station work. A riding school for Young Officers was held in the afternoon. The Commanding Officer and the Adjutant went with to G.O.C. 33rd.	

2353 Wt W2514/1454 700,000 5/15 D.D.&L. A.D.S.S./Forms/C. 2118.

WAR DIARY
or
INTELLIGENCE SUMMARY.
(Erase heading not required.)

Army Form C. 2118.

Place	Date	Hour	Summary of Events and Information	Remarks and references to Appendices
	1916 2nd June		Louvain. Orders received to complete amalgamation with the 5th Batt. by merging them up to establishment of officers & men. this was arranged for. All officers and men attached to the 1st Munsters and 1st Cameronians are to return to us to this again.	
	Saturday 3rd June		Officers and NCOs again paraded to the Lewis Gun and Grenades. Signalling Section paraded as usual. A School of Instruction for NCOs and also for return other than Signals, Lewis Gun & Grenades inaugurated this afternoon. Notes were received to return his 4 Lewis Guns to Ordnance. The day was warm. Major A.P. Graham returned from leave.	

WAR DIARY or INTELLIGENCE SUMMARY

Army Form C. 2118.

Place	Date	Hour	Summary of Events and Information	Remarks and references to Appendices
	1916 Sunday 4th June		The fields and men of the Battalion who were attached to the 18th Middlesex and 1st Remembrance returned to the Battalion today. A new report of the 4 companies Church Parade was held at 3pm to the field opposite Horse lines. The Kings Birthday Honours contained the following:— 6 M.G. for the Commanding Officer. Stars for 1600/Sgt Steane & R.R. Wilson. Military Medal for 1359 L/Cpl awarded a higher rate of pay under Quantum rate was also Article 241 R.W. The day was unsettled and very sultry.	

WAR DIARY or INTELLIGENCE SUMMARY

Army Form C. 2118.

Place	Date Hour	Summary of Events and Information	Remarks and references to Appendices
Monday BETHUNE	5th June 1916	The Adjutant and Captain Stewart attended 20Cth at to Majors of 33rd Div. Artillery. The Regt. Paraded from 9am to 12 noon and again from 2pm to 4pm. The school of instruction for young officers and NCOs Paraded as usual. All warrant officers & NCOs attended a lecture by the R.S.M. on "The Duties of NCOs". The day was dull and unsettled with a little sunshine occasionally.	
Tuesday 6th June		Boys Paraded for the Baths at GONNEHEM which we had been from 7.30 to 8.30 and the Regimental Exercises for all officers was held. All the officers proceeded to the ground and worked out 5 or 6 different tactical exercises. It was very interesting and instructive. The day was fair but showery.	

WAR DIARY or INTELLIGENCE SUMMARY

Army Form C. 2118.

Place	Date	Hour	Summary of Events and Information	Remarks and references to Appendices
1916	Wednesday 7th June		Boys paraded as per Programme of training for Close Order Drill. Extended Order Drill, Bayonet fighting in the Commanding Officer's judgement a boy in the afternoon and B Coy in the afternoon. Both Coys need and feel lacking order, and special attention too Given to getting the equipment in order. Lieut. Denholm returned from leave. Capt. Donaldson to Glasgow Highlanders. Rews left us for 7 Officers & N.C.Os 3 from 3/4 & 5 S.R. and 3 from to 3/4th 500 Rifles Received, a draft of Rifles. The day was spent as the day was programme of training for Close Order Drill. Extended Order Drill in the forenoon, the Commanding Officer inspected C Coy in the afternoon. Both Coys & Instruction Parades as usual Subaltern Officers attended	
Thursday 8th June		Boys paraded as per Boys paraded as per School at the new Subaltern Officers attended		

WAR DIARY or INTELLIGENCE SUMMARY

Army Form C. 2118.

Place	Date	Hour	Summary of Events and Information	Remarks and references to Appendices
1916	Friday 9 June		Companies paraded as per programme of training. In the afternoon orders were received that all Regimental Transport was to be transferred to 33rd Divisional Train, and Battalion instructed to prepare to move to Base. To arrange with 5th Scottish Rifles, Captain SINCLAIR (7th Sco. Rif.) and 2/Lts JOHNSTONE and WILSON (8th Sco. Rif.) were transferred to that Battalion.	[initials]
	Saturday 10 June		Companies route marched in forenoon. Orders were received for Battalion to entrain at CHOCQUES station for ETAPLES Base Depôt tomorrow afternoon. All transport was transferred today to 33rd Divisional Train. Some of the officers were very anxious to retain some of the Officers' Chargers, but permission to do so was not granted.	[initials]

Army Form C. 2118.

WAR DIARY
or
INTELLIGENCE SUMMARY.
(Erase heading not required.)

Place	Date	Hour	Summary of Events and Information	Remarks and references to Appendices
1916	Sunday 11 June		Orders are received that the Adjutant (Capt. D. L. GRAY) will not proceed to ETAPLES with the Battalion but will report to 19th Infy. Brigade for instruction. It is with much mutual regret that Capt. D. L. GRAY leaves the Battalion. The Commanding Officer appoints Capt. J.C.E. HAY as Adjutant. The Battalion entrains at CHOQUES station at 4.30 p.m. and after an exceedingly rapid journey for a French Railway System, detrains at ETAPLES station at about 9.45 p.m. Acquire Conducts the Battalion to the 37½. Infantry Base Depot, where the Battalion goes under Canvas.	
	Monday 12 June		This day is idle and wet. Coys are occupied in cleaning their respecting clothing equipment etc the	

Place	Date	Hour	Summary of Events and Information	Remarks and references to Appendices
1916.	Tuesday 13 June.		Commanding Officer and the Adjutant attended parade on Brig. General THOMSON, Base Commandant, Col. NASON, O.C. Reinforcements; and Col. COOK, O.C., 57th Infy. Base Dept. and formally reported the arrival of the Battalion. The Base Commandant instructed that the Battalion be paraded tomorrow in full marching order for inspection by himself. A draft of one officer (2/Lt. R.M. YOUNG) and certain other ranks are taken on the strength of the Battalion. The Battalion in full marching order was today inspected by the Base Commandant. There were on parade 32 Officers and 520 men, the largest Battalion	

WAR DIARY or INTELLIGENCE SUMMARY.

(Erase heading not required.)

Army Form C. 2118.

Place	Date	Hour	Summary of Events and Information	Remarks and references to Appendices
1916.				
			Parade since June 1915. The Base Commandant expressed himself as well pleased with the appearance of the Battalion. In the afternoon all NCO's and men were inspected medically by the Base Depot Medical Officer.	Appx
	Wednesday 14th June		Conference engage Groomen and afternoon in training as per Programme.	Appx
	Thursday 15th June		At 9.15 p.m. all clubs were more favourable and Training continued. A year ago today the Battalion took part in the fighting at FESTUBERT.	Appx
	Friday 16 June		Having continued in German Lines, Cambridge St. that Battalion now found 57th Infantry Base Depot to 34th Infantry Base Depot. Service completed by 5:30 p.m. Battalion again under Canvas. Eighteen Officers remained at 51st IBD as trained accommodation in 34th IBD was very limited.	Appx

2353 Wt. W2514/1434 700,000 5/15 D.D.&L. A.D.S.S./Forms/C. 2118.

WAR DIARY
or
INTELLIGENCE SUMMARY.
(Erase heading not required.)

Army Form C. 2118.

Place	Date	Hour	Summary of Events and Information	Remarks and references to Appendices
1916	Saturday 17 June		Training carried out in forenoon. In afternoon a fatigue party of 200 men was supplied for pitching tents to be occupied by Battalion tonight. Arrangements were made whereby 1100 other ranks otherwise not better the day was Warm & fine.	J.F.
	Sunday 18 June		Church Parade was held in the Scottish Churches Hut at 11 am. The Rev. H. MILLER of Edinburgh officiated. The afternoon was free of duties. In the small hours day the Battalion other than Twentieth to furnish at the shortest notice a party of one officer and 20 other ranks, who had to called upon to proceed to the assistance of french troops at any giving place. This party was instructed stages times today & any advantage will to be so instructed each day of out time of duty	J.F.

Army Form C. 2118.

WAR DIARY
or
INTELLIGENCE SUMMARY.
(Erase heading not required.)

Instructions regarding War Diaries and Intelligence Summaries are contained in F. S. Regs., Part II. and the Staff Manual respectively. Title pages will be prepared in manuscript.

Place	Date	Hour	Summary of Events and Information	Remarks and references to Appendices
1916	Monday 19 June		The Companies were engaged in transport and route marching during the morning and afternoon. The afternoon was free to enable the men to attend a boxing tournament in the Camp	Appx
	Tuesday 20 June		During the morning, firing and route marching. A Coy. sentries tent engaged training and route marching. A Coy. sentries tent. Doctor Lyon Gresfort	Appx
	Wednesday 21 June		B Coy. sentries tent. Bands in morning. During the morning Coy. was at disposal of Coy. Commander for Kit inspections etc. In the afternoon 200 men paraded & were marched to the sands at PARIS-PLAGE for bathing	Appx
	Thursday 22 June Friday 23 June		These two days were spent at training in vicinity of Camp. On 23rd Col. W.M.KAY was granted ten days leave to proceed home with a view to effecting the proper amalgamation of the "B" element with the 8th Sco. Rif.	Appx
	Saturday 24 June		This day was spent with no parades was possible during the forenoon. In the afternoon our arrangements were made	Appx

Place	Date	Hour	Summary of Events and Information	Remarks and references to Appendices

Sunday 25 June.

Windy misty wet weather hot baths. Also the whole Battalion paraded in the evening & worked under 'Setting in' at the Camp Lancaster.
The Commanding Officer (Major BOYD) inspected Coy lines. Church Parade Battalion held in the Scottish Church. Hut at 10.30 am. Service was conducted by Col. JAFFRAY.
This day was very hot and met Knight J.

Monday 26 June.

The Battalion was paraded for Adjutant's Battalion Parade from 6.10 am to 7.10 am. Arrangements have been made to proceed in the evening in the Dunes & Sand hills to the SOUTH of PARIS-PLAGE, and owing to heavy rain during the Evening and afternoon this arrangement has cancelled Coys paraded for inspection & musketry in Coy lines.

WAR DIARY
or
INTELLIGENCE SUMMARY.
(Erase heading not required.)

Army Form C. 2118.

Place	Date	Hour	Summary of Events and Information	Remarks and references to Appendices
1916 Tuesday	27 June		To-day was spent with Companies busy at different of Coy Commanders during forenoon. In the afternoon arrangements were made whereby MOs obtained hot baths. In the course of the morning the following extract from letter no A/10725/1 d/- 20/6/16 from A.G., G.H.Q. to D.A.G., 3rd Echelon was received:—	
			C.R. No 2425V C. "Officers of the 16th Scottish Rifles are posted as follows:—	
			Officers — Posted to	
			Capt J.C.G. May — 9th Bn Scottish Rifles Lieut H.R. McChristie — 1st Bn Scottish Rifles	
			Capt D.L. Gray — 1st " " 2/Lt. K.d. Muller — 5th do.	
			Capt I. Watt — 9th " " " C.I. Scott — 15th " Highland L.I.	
			Capt A.C. Stewart — 9th " " " W.R. Campbell — 10th " Scottish Rifles	
			Capt J.S. Hardie — 10th " " " G. Shearer — 8th " A. & S. Hrs.	
			Capt G. Mann — 10th " " " W.S. Mitchell — 8th " do.	
			Lieut G.W. Lawrie — 1st " " " W.L. Corbet — 8th " do.	
			Lieut R. Spiers — 5th " " " W.F. Brown — 5th " Scottish Rifles	
			Lieut J.M. Denholm — 1st " " " W. Weir — 6th " Seaforth Hrs.	

WAR DIARY
or
INTELLIGENCE SUMMARY.
(Erase heading not required.)

Army Form C. 2118.

Place	Date	Hour	Summary of Events and Information	Remarks and references to Appendices
			Officers Posted to	
			2/Lt J.W. Muirhead 6th Seaforth Hrs.	
			" R. Wilson 5th Scottish Rifles	
			" J. Ure 6th Seaforth Hrs.	
			" W. Sim 6th do.	
			" G.L. Dalzell 5th Scottish Rifles	
			Lieut & Q.M. J. Hamilton 1st Corps Cyclist Bn.	
			2/Lt W.D. Todd 11th Bn. A. & S. Hrs.	
			" D. Sorley 11th " do.	
			" E.F. Duncan 11th " do.	
			Capt. D. Sinclair 5th " Scottish Rifles	
			2/Lt W.J. Adam 5th " do	
			" J. Cruickshanks 5th " do	
			" R.M. Young 5th " do	
			" R. Millar 14th " A. & S. Hrs.	
			Lieut A.C. Wilson 14th " do	
			Officers Posted to	
			2/Lt R.W. Johnson 14th Bn A. & S. Hrs.	
			" J. Shearer 14th " do.	

WAR DIARY
or
INTELLIGENCE SUMMARY.
(Erase heading not required.)

Army Form C. 2118.

Place	Date	Hour	Summary of Events and Information	Remarks and references to Appendices
1916				
	Wednesday 28 June		On receipt of the letter Major Boyd & the Adjutant proceeded to Bt. Rouen and protested against the Officers being sent off to sea. As a result of same it was arranged that the Adjutant, Quarter Master and Junior Officers would not be called on immediately, but Funds reveals to remind up the Battalion. Instruction was also given that Major Boyd was ordered to the 1/5th Seaforth Highlanders and Major Graham to the 1/6th Seaforth Highlanders. Coys paraded in the morning for physical exercises & in the afternoon marched to PARIS-PLAGE for sea bathing parade. The afternoon was free. During the afternoon instructions were received for Major GRAHAM to proceed at 8.30 p.m. to join and take over the 6th B. Seaforth Highlanders. Major GRAHAM left at 8.30 p.m. – the beginning of the end.	
	Thursday 29 June		To-day was windy but dry. Companies paraded for training	

WAR DIARY or **INTELLIGENCE SUMMARY**
Army Form C. 2118.

Place	Date	Hour	Summary of Events and Information	Remarks and references to Appendices
1916.			In evening forming reformer. In the course of the day instructions were received that a nucleus of the Battalion would remain at the Base in which the Battalion orders to approved of some future date. Same would consist of 2 Officers (a Captain and Subaltern) and 50 other ranks. The latter to include the "Regimental Sergeant Major, Regt Quartermaster Sergeant, Sergeant "Piper, Orderly Room Clerk, and the Establishment of NCO's from "Hdqr Company." The names of the Sergeants (Col. Sjt. J.C.E. HAY) and Lieut. J.M. DENHOLM was submitted.	
Friday 30 June			Coys. paraded in morning for Physical exercises & in summer. Marched to sands beyond PARIS-PLAGE for bathing. Owing to the rain and wind this was not accomplished. In the afternoon Coys. were at disposal of O.C. Company for inspections.	
Saturday 1 July			In the early morning Coys. parades under the Subaltern. The Battalion Drill under the Adjutant during the forenoon. 3,450 other ranks paraded at ETAPLES to reach clothes, and	

L of C.
~~100th Inf. Bde.~~
~~33rd Div.~~

WAR DIARY

1/6th BATTN. THE CAMERONIANS (SCOTTISH RIFLES).

J U L Y

1 9 1 6

** 16th Scottish Rifles **

Vol 201

16.P
12 sheets

WAR DIARY
or
INTELLIGENCE SUMMARY.
(Erase heading not required.)

Army Form C. 2118.

Place	Date	Hour	Summary of Events and Information	Remarks and references to Appendices
1916				
	Sunday 2 July		The men had and a half in the afternoon Coys parades for short arms drill etc. The Battalion attended Church Parade at 10.30 am, the service was conducted by Col JAFFRAY. The Church Parade the Commanding Officer inspected Coy lines. The afternoon was free.	
	Monday 3 July		Coys. finished doing morning & afternoon afternoon for training officers. In the afternoon instruction was received that the following officers were to proceed early on the morning of 4th inst to join their new units :- Capt J. MAIN to 10th Sco R.y. Lt. H.R.M. CHRISTIE to 12th Sco R.y. 2/Lts. W.F.ADAM, G.G.DALZIEL, K.S.MILLER, W.F.BROWN, R.WILSON, J.CRUIKSHANK all to 5th Sco R.y.; 2/Lts. D.SORLEY and T.McTODD and E/L [?] DUNCAN to 11th A.S. Hqs.; 2/Lt. W.R. CAMPBELL to 70th Sco R.y. and 2/Lt.s R.MILLEN and T.SHEARER to 14th A.S. Hqs. Col. W.M.KAY returned from leave late this evening.	
	Tuesday 4 July		Instructions were received today regarding the remaining officers and the following officers departed for their new units in the course of the day :- Capt. T.WATT to 41st Sco R.y. 2/Lts. W.WEIR and T.URE	

T2134. Wt. W708-776. 500000. 4/15. Sir J.C.&S.

WAR DIARY or INTELLIGENCE SUMMARY

Army Form C. 2118.

(Erase heading not required.)

Instructions regarding War Diaries and Intelligence Summaries are contained in F. S. Regs., Part II. and the Staff Manual respectively. Title pages will be prepared in manuscript.

Place	Date	Hour	Summary of Events and Information	Remarks and references to Appendices
			to Lt. Seaford Hgtrs. and 2/Lt.s G. SHEARER and W.S. MITCHELL to 8th A. & S. Hgtrs. Lt.s G. SHEARER and W.S. MITCHELL also received that 2nd Lt. S.V. LAWRIE was ordered proceed to join the 4th Bn LONDON R.S.F. as Regimental Transport Officer, but same were cancelled later owing to that Battalion being on the move. Cups. received in forenoon and marched to PARIS-PLAGE for Sea training and in afternoon. Nothing further.	
Wednesday 5 July			Today the 13 station furnished a 24 hour guard of two officers and 100 other ranks for fatigue duty at the Base Detention Camp. Owing to the shortage of officers caused by the expiration too many of four bour kent duties, the Cm remaining in Camp Proceeded on a route march during the forenoon under the available officer. The afternoon was spent with the exception that 140 other ranks paraded for baths at the Russian Baths.	
Thursday 6 July			During the morning 40 Jammen the Cups. carried out physical exercises, it a route march. In the afternoon instruction were	

WAR DIARY or INTELLIGENCE SUMMARY.

Army Form C. 2118.

Place	Date	Hour	Summary of Events and Information	Remarks and references to Appendices
			received that about 250 other ranks were to be transferred forthwith to the 20th Inf. Base Depot – these Scottish Rifles Regimental Depot – to be used as reinforcements. 225 other ranks were so transferred, being the whole of A and B Coy. with the exception of some employed men. Orders were also received by Col. W.M. KAY to report at the War Office, LONDON forthwith and arrangements were made for Col. KAY's proceeding to ENGLAND on Sunday, 9th inst. 2/Lts MUIRHEAD and SIM reported back from leave.	Apps
	FRIDAY 7th July.		To-day was very wet indeed no training carried on. Procured with thirty four other ranks reported back from leave which have been greater than 8 others C.O. Seventeen other ranks were transferred to 20th Inf. Base Depot as reinforcements. In the evening instructions were received for 2nd Lt. R. SPIERS to proceed to Head Quarters, Royal Flying Corps as an Observer on probation	Apps
	Saturday 8th July.		To-day the remaining men went for a route march in the forenoon	

WAR DIARY or INTELLIGENCE SUMMARY

Army Form C. 2118.

Place	Date	Hour	Summary of Events and Information	Remarks and references to Appendices
1916			The chief was out. Warm night. In the evening instructions were received for Lt./On and J. HAMILTON to proceed early in the morning 9 q.t. to join 1st Corps Cyclist Battalion as Quarter Master.	
Sunday	9 July		This morning Col WM RAY left for ENGLAND and Lt./Qm J. HAMILTON left at 7am to join his Unit. Church Parade was held at 10.30 am under Col. JACKSON. Owing to the large call from the front for reinforcements all officers and men who were today competent to leave camp will probably be instructed not received for 7Kt. N. S/M to join the 6 & Gordon Highlanders by him leaving at 8.20 pm Instructions was also received for Lt. R.F. G.V. LAWRIE to join the 4th LONDON REGT. as Regimental Transport Officer in the evening	
Ripon	10		Instructions were received to furnish 200 Other ranks as reinforcements to 16th Bn. ROYAL SCOTS and 98 Other ranks to 1st/Bn. EAST YORKS Rgt. — detailed instructions under to follow tomorrow.	

WAR DIARY or INTELLIGENCE SUMMARY

Army Form C. 2118.

Place	Date	Hour	Summary of Events and Information	Remarks and references to Appendices
1916				
	Monday 10 July		The forenoon was spent in preparing the drafts called for. At 12.40 pm 200 other ranks from C & D Coys and 95 other ranks from A (which had already been warned to the 2nd 9.B.D.) proceeded to join the 6/1 Royal Scots and 1st East Yorks Regt. respectively. Capt J.C. HARDIE; Lt. J.M. DENHOLM and 2/Lt W.L. COOPER accompanied the two parties as Conducting Officers.	
	Tuesday 11 July		To day the tracking up of the Battalion was practically completed. Sixty other ranks were transferred to 20th 9.B.D. as reinforcements and the two Lewis Guns and two Lewis gun teams transferred to 51st & 9.B.D. for the same purpose. Of the Battalion there now remain only the nucleus of two Officers and 50 other ranks; the Armourer Staff Sergeant and this two Officers with Servants awaiting orders to join their new Battalions. Capt RAWLINS RAMP(?) is still remains with us, but not officially, as he has been	

T2134. Wt. W708-776. 500000. 4/15. Sir J. C. & S.

WAR DIARY or INTELLIGENCE SUMMARY.

Army Form C. 2118.

Appointed M.O. to two Bns. Details. The Officers, Warrant Officers, NCO's and men of the NUCLEUS are as follows:—

Captain Hay J.C.

Lieut. Denholm J.M.

Warrant Officers

3406	Regt. S.M.	Baldock	W.
321	Coy. S.M.	McCartney	J.

487	Regt. Q.M. Sgt.	Reid	D.
507	Coy. Q.M. Sgt.	McLellan	J.

N.C.O's

118	Sergeant	Brown	J.
958	"	Webster	W.
1861	"	Stewart	R.J.
1452	L/"	Stannage	J.
1439	Corporal	Hill	G.
1953	"	Stirrat	J.
1009	L/Corporal	Matheson	R.
1397	"	Ballantyne	R.

258	Sergeant	Greenshields	J.
2179	"	White	J.
1617	"	McDonald	A.
2101	Corporal	Connell	J.
1947	"	Kurland	J.
1470	"	Dolobwn	J.
1717	Lance Corporal	Fisher	L.
2181	"	Sharp	N.

Army Form C. 2118.

WAR DIARY
or
INTELLIGENCE SUMMARY.
(Erase heading not required.)

Instructions regarding War Diaries and Intelligence Summaries are contained in F. S. Regs., Part II. and the Staff Manual respectively. Title pages will be prepared in manuscript.

Place	Date	Hour	Summary of Events and Information	Remarks and references to Appendices
			2557 Lance Corporal McLean N.	
			1598 Bugler West J.	
			1199 " McMahon J.	
			221 Private Barclay J.	
			260 " Hannah W.	
			607 " Wright W.S.	
			821 " Douglas J.	
			1163 " Reid W.	
			1191 " Duncan J.	
			1360 " Ritchie A.	
			1457 " Potter J.	
			1588 " Worn J.	
			1828 " Clark J.	
			1650 " Robertson W	
			2401 " Logan J.	
			2180 Lance Corporal Watt W.	
			Moor	
			1625 Bugler Hawthorn J.	
			219 Private Arthur J.	
			231 " Clark J.	
			353 " Docherty W.	
			690 " Mair P.	
			1162 " Kreps R.	
			1167 " McVie E.	
			1357 " Douglas J.	
			1435 " Laird C.	
			1489 " Potter J.	
			1798 " Dobson R.	
			1603 " Ferrier R.	
			1546 " Hutchison R.	
			1499 " Potter J.	

T2134. Wt. W708—776. 500000. 4/15. Sir J. C. & S.

Army Form C. 2118.

WAR DIARY
or
INTELLIGENCE SUMMARY.
(Erase heading not required.)

Instructions regarding War Diaries and Intelligence Summaries are contained in F. S. Regs., Part II. and the Staff Manual respectively. Title pages will be prepared in manuscript.

Place	Date	Hour	Summary of Events and Information	Remarks and references to Appendices
1916	Wednesday 12 July.		The morning was finished in moving Transport overseers and rank and file. Lt. DENHOLM I/cer 2/Lt COOPER returned to Camp having handed over the 200 other ranks allotted to the 16th Royal Scots who were billeted at HENENCOURT.	
	Thursday 13 July.		Available men paraded in morning. 7 men (or Physical exercises and rank and file. 128 other ranks (7 men B.O. Cpr) proceeded today in reinforcements to 9th Scottish Rifles, and the Armourer Staff Sergeant was ordered to proceed to CALAIS to report to 10c Ordnance Companies.	
	Friday 14 July		All the men of the number have either been given special work to do in the D.3rd A.B.D. or have been attached to the Regiment Bugler to complete his Brigade Band. All ranks will be inspected each morning & thought will be engaged on their own special employments.	
	Saturday 15 July		Today arrangements were made for hot baths and having clothes washed	

WAR DIARY
or
INTELLIGENCE SUMMARY.
(Erase heading not required.)

Army Form C. 2118.

Place	Date	Hour	Summary of Events and Information	Remarks and references to Appendices
	1916			
	Sunday 16 July		All ranks paraded for Church Service at 10.30 am which was conducted by Col. JAFFRAY.	
	Monday 17		No event worthy of special mention occurring until Tuesday morning when the Adjutant was instructed to attend at HQrs. O.C. Reinforcements.	
	Tuesday 18		Instructions were there given to the effect that the Draken under late our a Depot numbered "W.2" from the NEW SEALAND Contingent as soon as possible. She is at present at the staff for running the Depot should be furnished by the Draken, and same would be met by O.C. Reinforcements for an overflow from the Depot. They to arrangements were made with the N.Z. Contingent that the Depot should be partially vacated to nurses, and empty rooms to be as soon as possible thereafter. An account for the necessary stores etc. was submitted to the COO. which he refused to grant, and the position of affairs was brought before me to Col. NASON (O.C. Reinforcements.)	

T.134. Wt. W708-776. 500000. 4/15. Sir J.C. & S.

WAR DIARY or INTELLIGENCE SUMMARY

Army Form C. 2118.

Place	Date	Hour	Summary of Events and Information	Remarks and references to Appendices
1916				
	Wed 19 July		This morning the Battalion strength transferred from 34th G.B.D. to "Z" Depot, which had been partially vacated by the N.Z. Contingent. Same was reported to O.C. Regiment and further instructions awaited. In the afternoon orders were given to Major J. BOYD and Capt A.C. STEWART to proceed to join Otto 5th Bn. Seaforth Highrs and 9th Scottish Rifles, respectively, and also two officers in advance at 5 p.m.	
	Thursday 20 July	8	Today Lt Col. Scott, 2/Lt J.W. MUIRHEAD and 2/Lt W.L. COOPER proceeded to join the 7/5 & 7/6 A.& S.H., the 6th Seaforth Highrs and the 8th A. & S. 14 gdrs respectively. The N.C.O's and men of the drawn was allotted centre in the administration of Z depot and arrangements were made whereby certain detachments of the NEW ZEALAND Depot should continue to carry on in Z depot, in the meantime.	
	Friday 21 July		Today 203 other ranks from 18 & 9.B.D. were transferred to Z depot. They consisted of Black Watch, Gordon and Seaforth reinforcements.	
	Saturday 22 July		Today a further detachment of 150 Seaforths were transferred to	

Army Form C. 2118.

WAR DIARY
or
INTELLIGENCE SUMMARY.
(Erase heading not required.)

Instructions regarding War Diaries and Intelligence
Summaries are contained in F. S. Regs., Part II.
and the Staff Manual respectively. Title pages
will be prepared in manuscript.

Place	Date	Hour	Summary of Events and Information	Remarks and references to Appendices
	1916			
	Sunday 23 July		From 18&93.D the draft were sent to Harming Camp at Jarvering to order.	
		8	Today all available NCO's were of the various parades for Divine Service at 10.30 am. In the afternoon a draft of 100 troops were transferred to 2/8 the other drafts started Training Journal & were previously Inspected.	
	Monday 24	"	Drafts in Difft purades according to order.	
	Tuesday 25	"		
	Wednesday 26	"		
	Thursday 27		Instructions were today received that the Regiment would take over charge of a new temporary training camp at COUQ, & authority was granted him to obtain the necessary Instruction Arrangements were accordingly made for the transfer to 2 Dept. June 205. 9BD T.J. Havant Officers NCO's & the 20 Battalion who died Inst. got leave sent to men Wollaton in reinforcements Two other Instructors were detailed from 4th Canadian Regt.	

T2134. Wt. W708—776. 500000. 4/15. Sir J. C. & 8.

WAR DIARY
or
INTELLIGENCE SUMMARY.
(Erase heading not required.)

Army Form C. 2118.

Instructions regarding War Diaries and Intelligence Summaries are contained in F. S. Regs., Part II. and the Staff Manual respectively. Title pages will be prepared in manuscript.

Place	Date	Hour	Summary of Events and Information	Remarks and references to Appendices
1916.				
Ireland	Friday 28 July		5th Black Watch and 6th Royal Scots the Adjutant was also instructed to continue in charge of 2 Camp & funeral staff of same from Belfast Brushm Barracks attending at C800 g Thurrap Camp today 1915.	
	Saturday 29 "		1905. Brushes in 2 Camp 815.	
			6009 Brushes attending Camp 1271; Brushes in 2 Camp 994.	
			Do. 689 : do 994.	
	Sunday 30 "		Brushm parades to-day for Divine Service at 10.30. do 994.	

Army Form C. 2118.

6 Scottish Rifles

Vol 2

WAR DIARY
or
INTELLIGENCE SUMMARY.
(Erase heading not required.)

17. P.
1 sheet

Place	Date	Hour	Summary of Events and Information	Remarks and references to Appendices
	August 1916		During the month of August the NUCLEUS of the Battalion continued to form the Staff of "2" Camp, ETAPLES. Various numbers of men were taken on the strength of the Camp – the highest number during the month being 3035. No outstanding event worthy of record occurred during the month.	J Gyffe

Army Form C. 2118.

WAR DIARY
or
INTELLIGENCE SUMMARY.   6th Bn Yorks Regt
(Erase heading not required.)

Vol 2

6th Bn Yorks Rifles

Instructions regarding War Diaries and Intelligence Summaries are contained in F. S. Regs., Part II. and the Staff Manual respectively. Title pages will be prepared in manuscript.

Place	Date	Hour	Summary of Events and Information	Remarks and references to Appendices
1916 September October			During the months of September and October the Battalion continued to do statistical work at ETAPLES Base.

 R Oakley Capt. O/C Northern Cyclists | |

Appx Vol 27

WAR DIARY
or
INTELLIGENCE SUMMARY.
(Erase heading not required.) (NUCLEUS) 6th Bn.

Army Form C. 2118.

The Cameronians (Scottish Rifles)

Place	Date	Hour	Summary of Events and Information	Remarks and references to Appendices
	1916. November December 1917 January		During these months the Nucleus of the Battalion continued to be stationed at ETAPLES Base.	

Lieut. G. Hay Capt.
O/C Nucleus 6th Cam: R.

O.C. Reinforcements. Confidential

Will you please investigate, and call on the O.C of the Unit concerned as to why the Diary was rendered in this Form. The allusion to "Z" Camp is not clear. Was not this Camp occupied by the New Zealand Division prior to the date named?

Etaples 19.1.17

G.D. White. Major
D.A.A. M.G.

O.C.
1/6. Scottish Rifles

With reference to the above minute please explain why this Diary was rendered in such a vague manner.

MAJOR.
D.A.A.G. REINFORCEMENTS.

19 JAN 1917

D.A.A.G.
Reinforcements.

CONFIDENTIAL.

     It is explained, please, that, as has always been the practice with this Unit, the attached Diary was rendered to G.H.Q. 3rd. Echelon under cover of a Confidential Memo explaining that it referred to this Unit.

     Diary is returned amended, please.

21/1/17.
"L" Camp.

Captain,
O.C. 6th. Scottish Rifles.

CONFIDENTIAL

A.G.'s OFFICE AT THE BASE.
War Diaries & Records.
DATE...........
C. R. No. 140/1801

Base Commandant
Staples

The attached War Diary is forwarded to you, having been received with nothing on it to show to what Unit in the B.E.F. it refers.

It is believed to belong to a Unit under your Command Division, and if this is the case please issue instructions to prevent War Diaries being submitted in such a manner that it is impossible to identify them.

General Headquarters,
3rd Echelon,
13 / 1916

Major-General,
D. A. G.

CONFIDENTIAL.

D.A.G.,
   G.H.Q., 3rd Echelon.

Forwarded.

Etaples.   Brigadier-General,
23.1.17.   Commandant.

SENT HERE IN ERROR

CONFIDENTIAL.

The A.A & Q.M.J
"No 2" E.A.D.

Amended diary from O.C nucleus 6th Scottish Rifles
herewith.

22.1.17

F.J Mason COLONEL.
COMDG. REINFORCEMENTS, ETAPLES.

www.ingramcontent.com/pod-product-compliance
Lightning Source LLC
Chambersburg PA
CBHW081247170426
43191CB00037B/2073